Foreword

Welcome to the new ISTE Standards for Coaches, your road map to the characteristics, activities, philosophies and dispositions of today's instructional technology coaches, as well as those needed for future practice in this evolving role.

These standards, developed through close investigation of the learning sciences and with input from thousands of educators around the globe, strive to ensure that learning with technology is high-impact, sustainable, scalable and equitable for all. The result is a set of standards that help define the role of the coach; show how it relates to the roles addressed in the ISTE Standards for Students, Educators, and Education Leaders; and discuss the role as it relates to the ISTE Essential Conditions.

Change Agent. Connected Learner. Collaborator. Learning Designer. Professional Learning Facilitator. Data-Driven Decision-Maker. Digital Citizen Advocate.

The very names of the new Coaching Standards point to the many and varied roles coaches take on and to the diverse nature of their responsibilities in supporting their education colleagues.

Use this guide to get a deep understanding of each of the standards, tips for applying them to practice and reflections on the pivotal role coaches play in transforming teaching and learning.

Thank you to the thousands of educators who contributed to the new Coaching Standards. Your input was invaluable to the creation of these standards that are sure to empower coaches worldwide.

Richard Culatta
ISTE CEO

Contents

Introduction

The instructional technology coach is the critical lever in ensuring high-impact transformational learning with digital technology. The effective coach, personified in the ISTE Standards for Coaches, is the person who empowers and inspires educators, education leaders and students to harness technology to improve pedagogy and reach higher learning goals. The coach's role has dramatically evolved since this position was initially implemented in schools. The ISTE Standards for Coaches (2019), reflect the characteristics, activities, philosophies and dispositions of today's instructional technology coach and those needed for future practice in this evolving role.

These standards were developed through close investigation of the learning sciences of how students and adults learn, and with research evidence and practitioner experience on effective practices, to ensure that learning with technology is high-impact learning that's sustainable, scalable and equitable for all.

The Evolving Role of the Instructional Technology Coach

The inclusion of digital technology had a destabilizing effect on educational approaches in traditional schools and classrooms. As early technologies seeped from the surrounding society into schools, a need emerged for someone to guide how, when and why to incorporate technology into the curriculum. Educational strategies and methods had to be examined. This led to the role of the technology facilitator in schools. This role has greatly changed over a relatively short time. This evolution of the role of coach can be seen in the ISTE Standards for Coaches (2019), which followed the ISTE Standards for Coaches (2011) and the ISTE Standards for Technology Facilitators (2001). Across schools and districts, the role of coach has been reimagined several times due to changes in teaching strategies, technology, society and new knowledge from the learning sciences. These changes can be broadly categorized as three phases. See Figure 1.

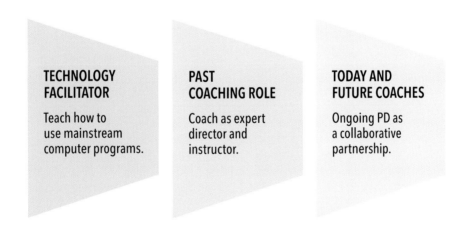

TECHNOLOGY FACILITATOR

Teach how to use mainstream computer programs.

PAST COACHING ROLE

Coach as expert director and instructor.

TODAY AND FUTURE COACHES

Ongoing PD as a collaborative partnership.

Figure 1. The Changing Role of Instructional Technology Coach.

Phase One: Technology Facilitator

The early thinking was that teachers could be supported by showing them how to use well-publicized programs, such as Microsoft Excel and PowerPoint. By teaching them to use these tools, they would be able to show students how to use them. This technocentric phase lasted for a few years before it became clear that this model was not working, as educators were not implementing technology in the classroom.

Phase Two: Past Coaching Role

The name shifted to coach from the business and management sector (Smither & Reilly, 2001) as it was recognized that educators needed higher quality professional development. The focus was on the role of the technology coach to show teachers how to consider technology alongside teaching practice. This was a major change in thinking as this was connecting technology and pedagogy. However, this approach was one of the technology coach as the director of learning. The coach would inform the teachers of what strategy and technology they should be using and support teachers in doing that. This included developing and maintaining communication with teachers, managing assessment and materials and conducting training sessions (Rivera, Burley, & Sass, 2004). The focus was often in support of current school/district initiatives and reforms.

Phase Three: Today and Future Coaches

This final phase involves a great many changes that include research-based best practices on adult learning for effective professional development that causes a shift in practices, philosophies, goals and dispositions of instructional technology coaches. The shift resulted from a better understanding of job-embedded professional development and research showing that situational learning activities successfully transform teaching (Wesely & Plummer, 2007). This brought about more modeling and collaborative supportive practices. This coach works in collaboration with both educators and educational leaders, listening to their needs and developing relevant professional development opportunities. This coach also uses iterative, cyclical coaching frameworks to provide ongoing support and development strategies. Table 1 provides an overview of the shifting role of the technology coach.

Table 1. Three Phases in the Changing Role of the Technology Coach

Phase One Technology Facilitator	Phase Two Past Coaching Role	Phase Three Today and Future Coaches
Direct coaching	Direct coaching	Collaborative coaching
One-and-done training	One-and-done training	Iterative cyclical process of professional development
Focus on preparing educators to use programs	Focus on initiatives and reforms	Focus on PD needs of individual educators and education leaders
PD for educators	PD for educators	PD for educators and education leaders

The ISTE Standards for Coaches (2019) take into account these new understandings, providing a set of seven standards with indicators that give specific examples of what it looks like for a coach to meet each standard. The standards include factors that ensure they remain up to date and relevant. The ISTE Standards for Coaches are goals for coaches to reach to ensure they're supporting educators, education leaders and students in using technology for high-impact practices.

Characterizing the Coaching Standards

This section of the booklet unpacks each of the seven standards to outline the meaning behind the text. This will help educators understand the standards and how to best apply them to their practice.

As you read this section, it is important to know that the standards are made up of the standard statement, which is the initial sentence, and the indicators, which is the additional text listed by number. The standard provides an overarching statement of what the educators will be doing if they are effectively integrating technology into teaching and learning. The indicators provide concrete skill sets that demonstrate mastery of the standard.

1. Change Agent

Coaches inspire educators and leaders to use technology to create equitable and ongoing access to high-quality learning. Coaches:

a. Create a shared vision[1] and culture for using technology to learn and accelerate transformation through the coaching process[2].

b. Facilitate equitable use of digital learning tools[3] and content that meet the needs of each learner.

c. Cultivate a supportive coaching culture[4] that encourages educators and leaders to achieve a shared vision and individual goals.

d. Recognize educators[5] across the organization who use technology effectively to enable high-impact teaching and learning[6].

e. Connect[7] leaders, educators, instructional support, technical support, domain experts and solution providers[8] to maximize the potential of technology[9] for learning.

---

1. **Create a shared vision:** Work together with common purpose and foresight to visualize the full potential of technology to transform teaching and learning.

2. **Coaching process:** A cycle of improvement for working with educators to set goals, plan, implement and reflect; *(see research for evidence-based frameworks or models).*

3. **Equitable use of digital learning tools and content:** Access to resources educators can use to expand high-impact learning opportunities for students (e.g., experiential learning vs. memorization); meeting the needs of learners regardless of their ability, gender, ethnicity, socio-economic status, language or physical needs.

4. **Supportive coaching culture:** For example, building relationships with educators and leaders where a coach is approachable, accessible, available and nonevaluative.

5. **Recognize educators:** Showcase educators and their classroom projects to serve as models for others.

6. **High-impact teaching and learning:** Learning is designed with student outcomes in mind, and instruction is grounded in pedagogical research and the learning sciences.

7. **Connect:** Serve as liaison between stakeholders to carry out the vision and solve problems.

8. **Solution providers:** Vendors who offer tools or professional learning for an education audience.

9. **Maximize potential of technology:** Purposefully use tools, functionality and methods to best meet the needs of learners and deepen their mastery of learning concepts

Effective coaches engender a school culture that embraces the positive potential of student learning. Digital tools are a powerful force in the classroom and offer the potential to shift from traditional teaching approaches. This can evoke fear in some educators. This fear is recognized by the coach who works to develop a nurturing environment with a shared vision of why technology is used and the value it has in helping meet learning goals. The coach works closely with educators to support them in developing goals and understanding that digital potential. Teachers with successful technology stories are highlighted to provide a concrete example for other educators and honor the dedication of those educators.

With any positive tool or intervention, the Matthew effect, the idea that the rich get richer and the poor get poorer, is often a concern. Effective coaches ensure that all students have the same opportunities and benefits of using technology for enhancing and extending teaching and learning. Historically, socio-economic status was the major and often primary concern for acknowledging a disparity in learning opportunities with technology. Today's coaches are highly aware of other student groups who may miss out on what digital technologies can offer. Effective coaches create equitable access for all students, regardless of socio-economic status, learner level, race, gender, physical ability, primary language and computer literacy. Coaches are also continually on the lookout for other factors that may inhibit student accessibility to technology that may not have been anticipated.

The coach acts as a change agent in bringing leaders, educators, instructional support, technical support, domain experts and solution providers to work together with a common goal of using technology to help learners reach their potential and accomplish their dreams.

Effective coaches don't just look who is left behind, but also who is left on the side.

There are five indicators that provide useful concrete examples to accompany this standard. The first indicator has the coach as change agent as they create a shared vision and culture for technology use. The second has the coach ensuring digital learning access for all learners. The third indicator focuses on a supportive coaching culture that has both educators and leaders successfully developing and achieving a shared vision and individual technology goals. The fourth indicator has effective coaches highlighting educators who are using technology to transform learning and showing high learning achievement. The fourth indicator is coach in the role of connected facilitator in bringing strategic people together to gain the greatest benefits from digital instruction.

Here are examples of how ISTE members connect with this standard:

As an instructional technology coach, I provide opportunities for teachers and students to equitably access resources and use digital learning tools. To help leverage the learning of students with various abilities and language levels, I work one-to-one with teachers. I help design instruction and co-teach/model lessons that allow students of all backgrounds to engage in and experience the learning in an impactful way. A critical component of equity is that all students get the opportunity to use technology that supports higher-order thinking, not just memorizing facts.

— Angela Rowe, Virginia

I hold "Curiosity Café" gatherings monthly to bring together teachers to maximize the potential of technology. During these times, we stay focused on topics that teachers are curious about and want to explore. We discuss how and where they can redefine lessons with apps, websites and articles that deepen student learning of content. This cafe offers teachers the opportunity to truly explore impactful technology as a group. We also allow time for implementation and reflection.

— Ashley Read, Texas

2. Connected Learner

Coaches model the ISTE Standards for Students and the ISTE Standards for Educators and identify ways to improve their coaching practice. Coaches:

a. Pursue professional learning that deepens expertise in the ISTE Standards in order to serve as a model[1] for educators and leaders.

b. Actively participate in professional learning networks[2] to enhance coaching practice and keep current with emerging technology[3] and innovations in pedagogy[4] and the learning sciences[5].

c. Establish shared goals[6] with educators, reflect on successes and continually improve coaching and teaching practice.

New digital tools are constantly appearing hand in hand with new approaches to teaching to take advantage of these new tools. It's important for coaches to be constantly learning and open to new avenues of inquiry. Research shows that learning happens most when you're connected with other people and resources. Being a connected learner means that you seek out ways to extend your knowledge and model what this looks like to others, such as administrators, educators and students.

1. **Model:** Individuals who intentionally and transparently adopt and demonstrate best practices.

2. **Professional learning networks:** Virtual, blended learning or in-person communities, like professional learning communities.

3. **Emerging technology:** New technologies or using existing technology in new ways.

4. **Innovations in pedagogy:** Shifts in teaching and learning, such as increased personalization and differentiation; real-time or asynchronous collaboration; authentic projects with experts and real-world data; providing immediate feedback using digital tools; competency-based assessments and data analysis tools.

5. **Learning sciences:** An interdisciplinary field bringing together findings from research into cognitive, social and cultural psychology, neuroscience and learning environments, among others, with the goal of implementing learning innovations and improving instructional practice.

6. **Shared goals:** A set of mutually agreed upon objectives that guide collaborative work.

Technology is changing at a rapid pace, as are the new teaching approaches provided by the technologies. Coaches cannot possibly know everything there is to know about all the tools and approaches. However, they can keep abreast of changes and, if they have a question they can't answer, they can model excellent learner strategies. These strategies include reaching out to their professional learning networks using hashtags and keywords to gain pertinent speedy responses, conducting internet searches using search strategies and knowing where to look for answers.

> ## We don't have to have the answer to everything, we just need to be connected to those that do.

The three indicators provide concrete ways to become a connected learner. The first is a call to action to actively pursue professional learning – to consider what knowledge and skills you need to grow as a coach and find access to that learning. The second indicator directs you onto the path of finding that learning, as effective coaches are active in professional learning networks. They engage in a dialogue to learn from, learn with, and share knowledge and skills with peers and experts to better understand shifts in learning and the learning sciences. The third indicator has coaches establishing shared goals with educators to extend and enhance learning.

Here are examples of how ISTE members connect with this standard:

> As a connected learner, I try to stay abreast of current educational trends – there are so many that this is a hard thing to do, so I use strategies. I look to Twitter, a few trusted blogs and ISTE message boards regularly so that I can identify topics that are trending. I participate in a few Twitter chats regularly, or check the archives when I miss them, so that I can see how others are addressing topics. I also look to the feedback surveys from professional development so that I can coordinate to find topics that are of interest to participants. I turn to my PLN to see if there are new techniques or studies that would change the way I could address the need for the requested PD.
>
> — Ruth Okoye, Washington, D.C.

> I analyze, reflect and advocate for the use of the ISTE Standards to provide a shared language during teacher professional development courses as we work as partners. I inspire participating educators to reflect on their own practices, and together we choose shared goals of technology use.
>
> — Juan Carlos López, Colombia

3. Collaborator

Coaches establish productive relationships with educators in order to improve instructional practice and learning outcomes. Coaches:

- **a.** Establish trusting and respectful coaching relationships[1] that encourage educators to explore new instructional strategies[2].
- **b.** Partner with educators to identify digital learning content[3] that is culturally relevant[4], developmentally appropriate and aligned to content standards.
- **c.** Partner with educators to evaluate the efficacy[5] of digital learning content and tools to inform procurement decisions and adoption[6].
- **d.** Personalize support for educators by planning and modeling the effective use of technology to improve student learning[7].

Healthy relationships are those built on mutual caring and empowerment. Effective coaches recognize the power of productive relationships and work toward building strong connections with the educators they serve. For coaches to make the greatest impact on the school, they recognize that trust between the coach and the educator/leader/students is at the very core of the relationships. For example, educators have to feel comfortable to try out new ideas and technologies, knowing they have the support, encouragement and empowerment from the coach, even when it fails. Coaches recognize the power dynamic that exists between their high level of expertise in technology and others they work with who often have lesser expertise, in addition to the expertise the educator has in content knowledge that the coach is often missing. It's important that educators feel they're not being judged, but are being encouraged. Coaches show support by working together, supporting educators in working toward implementing the ISTE Standards for Educators and the ISTE Standards for Students. Educators should understand that they will not always get everything right and "failing forward" is part of the learning process. Collaboratively, the coach and the educator will learn together.

---

1. **Coaching relationships:** Dispositions that strengthen the working relationship between coaches and educators, such as social-emotional awareness, self-awareness, a sense of ethics and integrity, active listening and effective communication.

2. **Explore new instructional strategies:** Learn, try out and iterate a variety of proven, promising and emerging instructional strategies.

3. **Digital learning content:** A broad range of learning materials available via devices, such as digital media and podcasts; digital curriculum, news and websites; digitized original or historical resources; and virtual field trips or virtual reality.

4. **Culturally relevant:** Content that reflects the multicultural nature of society.

5. **Efficacy of digital learning content and tools:** Establishing that a particular tool or content achieves intended learning outcome, based on research and evidence.

6. **Procurement decisions and adoption:** Process to evaluate and make decisions about purchasing edtech solutions that may address efficacy, the learning sciences, interoperability, privacy, etc., and once decisions are made, incorporating selected resources into regular practice and workflows.

7. **Effective use of technology:** An approach that supports student mastery of content knowledge while also gaining vital competencies, including problem-solving, critical thinking, effective communication, collaboration and self-direction.

Effective coaches practice what they preach as they model good teaching approaches with the use of digital technologies. This modeling is a great way to show educators not only how to use new approaches and technology, but it also provides context to demonstrate how students react and what happens during all parts of the process. Educators may not be fearful of how to use the technology, but rather what it will look like in practice with students. With the coach working collaboratively with the educator, it provides a feeling of accomplishment as the educator is part of the process. There's also a sense of safety, as they're working with someone who has knowledge, skills and passion to learn from. Effective coaches are highly aware that educators are the content experts and a collaborative process of sharing expertise is necessary to determine what technologies work best to deepen content learning. A two-way line of communication is used to determine procurement and adoption decisions. The coach empowers the educator to use their content expertise and personal knowledge of the students to match good practices, strategies and tools to meet the needs of all learners.

 Take calculated risks together. Failure and reflection is a vital part of the learning process.

Four indicators accompany this standard. The first focuses on building a coaching relationship based on trust and respect. The second has the coach and educator identifying digital content that is culturally relevant, developmentally appropriate and aligned to content standards. In the third indicator, coaches and educators examine the effectiveness of digital content and tools that determine purchasing and adoption decisions. Finally, indicator four has coaches working with educators to plan and model effective technology use.

Here are examples of how ISTE members connect with this standard:

> I oversee four district instructional technology coaches. I'm their coach and their support. I have established trusting and respectful relationships with them to become district leaders. Each coach is responsible for 13–14 schools. Our entire office became ISTE certified. I have made it a priority to release district responsibility to them to become digital learning leaders so they can coach teachers. I encourage them to think outside the box and take risks with their learning and their workshop offerings. I don't say "no," I say, "try it and let's see if it works.
>
> — Sarah Kyriazis, Massachusetts

> Each year, our teachers are asked to set goals. In our coaching model, their goals are personal and it's one of our main initiatives to guide and support teachers in their specific goal through trainings or just encouragement. We set up one-to-one meetings depending on the training needed; small groups if there are a few with similar goals, or even co-teaching lessons together for a gradual release of understanding for independence. In the next few weeks, we'll be offering a choice session where I and the two other district coaches will have three different 20-minute offerings for teachers to choose from during our Wednesday weekly collaboration meetings, which are similar to PLCs.
>
> — Dawn Jones, Florida

4. Learning Designer

Coaches model and support educators to design learning experiences and environments to meet the needs and interests of all students. Coaches:

a. Collaborate with educators to develop authentic, active learning experiences[1] that foster student agency[2], deepen content mastery and allow students to demonstrate their competency[3].

b. Help educators use digital tools to create effective assessments that provide timely feedback and support personalized learning[4].

c. Collaborate with educators to design accessible and active digital learning environments that accommodate learner variability[5].

d. Model the use of instructional design principles[6] with educators to create effective digital learning environments[7].

Strong learning design is paramount to effective teaching and learning. The design of learning requires drawing from past knowledge and experiences while thinking about strategies to meet the needs of all students. This standard encourages coaches to develop a collaborative working relationship with educators, allowing them to reflect on successful pedagogical strategies and current research to ensure the experience and environment they provide is effective for all types of learners.

Educators can often feel overwhelmed by all the pedagogical strategies and technologies that are pushed in their direction as the new latest and greatest. Coaches support educators in managing this influx of information by providing key focus areas to address. Coaches point educators in the direction of authentic and active learning experiences to provide learners with context and purpose. Active participation supports learning in committing learning to deep memory, allowing strong recall of skills and knowledge.

---

1. **Authentic, active learning experiences:** Experiential learning activities that are designed based on students' real-world experiences and interests, current issues or real data, and are implemented in a way that engages students (e.g., hands-on, debates, field work, etc.).

2. **Student agency:** A level of autonomy and self-direction from students taking responsibility and ownership of learning goals.

3. **Demonstrate their competency:** A variety of ways for students to demonstrate their knowledge, skills and dispositions, such as allowing them to choose a pace, schedule or work product/ artifact.

4. **Support personalized learning:** Capitalize on technology's efficiencies and functionality to develop assessments that meet students' individual learning needs using tools like scaled tests and quizzes; adaptability features; software that can capture where students are struggling or spending the bulk of their time; competency-based learning resources; and student reflection tools.

5. **Learner variability:** If planned for and supported, maximizes student learning and engagement, such as differentiation, assistive technologies, building motivation to learn by stimulating interest, multimodal content delivery, fostering learning awareness of their work preferences and recognition of how academic work aligns to personal goals.

6. **Instructional design principles:** Established and evolving best practices and guidelines for designing learning experiences for specific learners.

7. **Digital learning environments:** Online or virtual learning environments that use technology in the classroom to deliver content, personalize learning and manage student progress toward learning objectives.

Effective coaches also work with educators to ensure that learning design meets the needs of all learners. This includes thinking about the academic knowledge and skills of each student, learner preferences and differences in learning needs connected to language, culture and gender, and physical, cognitive and behavioral special needs. The coach models various strategies that the educator can replicate or even adapt further to meet the needs of their students.

Taking time to design effective learning is a demonstration that you care enough about all students to make learning relevant and accessible to all.

There are four indicators to accompany this standard. Each of these indicators provide concrete examples of what a coach would look like as they embody the Learning Designer standard. In this standard, the indicators are dense and have multiple components. Establish goals for yourself broken into manageable chunks. You do not have to cover every point in one lesson.

The first indicator highlights the need for a partnership with educators to design learning. This indicator highlights authentic and active learning experience as two pedagogical aims to increase student agency as well as develop content mastery. The second indicator covers how to create assessments with technology to provide students with speedy feedback and connect with personalized learning strategies. The third indicator has coaches fostering collaborative relationships with educators to develop digital learning environments that meet the needs of all learners. The final indicator addresses instructional design. As more learning environments are blended or fully digital, it becomes important for coaches and educators to know and apply good digital design principles for effective learning.

Here are examples of how ISTE members connect with this standard:

> I consider every professional learning engagement with teachers an opportunity to model effective blended learning instruction for them. Every interaction looks different based on the teachers I'm working with and the goals of the session. I want to ensure that every learning opportunity I provide incorporates learner choice, is highly interactive and engaging, and facilitates discussion, collaboration and application of the new skills. Teachers should walk away energized and excited about the learning opportunities for their students; then we're able to extend our work with teachers by helping them create resources and experiences that they learned with us.
>
> — Katie Ritter, Ohio

> As a technology mentor, I recognize the importance of designing and creating activities and learning environments that allow students to develop the skills necessary for meaningful learning. Sharing and modeling experiences and learning tools with educators will help them develop learning and create collaborative and social environments, and will also allow them to learn from their own learning processes. By applying the principles of instructional design to create such learning environments and adapting the content to the students' learning needs, I facilitate and promote meaningful learning, applying the principles of instructional design to create such learning environments and adapt the content to the students' learning needs we will be facilitating and promoting meaningful learning.
>
> — Rosa Morales, Puerto Rico

5. Professional Learning Facilitator

Coaches plan, provide and evaluate the impact of professional learning for educators and leaders to use technology to advance teaching and learning. Coaches:

a. Design professional learning based on needs assessments[1] and frameworks for working with adults[2] to support their cultural, social-emotional and learning needs[3].

b. Build the capacity of educators, leaders and instructional teams to put the ISTE Standards into practice by facilitating active learning[4] and providing meaningful feedback[5].

c. Evaluate the impact of professional learning[6] and continually make improvements in order to meet the schoolwide vision for using technology for high-impact teaching and learning.

Effective coaches embrace their roles as professional learning facilitators. This is a multidimensional role, and coaches understand the dynamic, interactive nature among educators, leaders and students. Coaches work with adult learners who are serving their students in the classroom and leaders who are serving the wider school, with the end goal of extending student learning with technology. To ensure the goal is met requires coaches to conduct iterative, cyclical evaluations on the professional learning provided to educators and leaders. Coaches need to confirm that educators and leaders are accessing relevant, accessible content that provides the greatest impact on the adult learner to make the greatest difference to K–12 students.

---

1. **Needs assessments:** A systematic approach for identifying areas for professional learning and assessing the capacity to meet those needs.

2. **Frameworks for working with adults:** Theories for working with adults, developing learning objectives based on learners' needs, providing a process for achieving those objectives, creating opportunities for learner choice and evaluating learners' progress (see *research for evidence-based models*).

3. **Cultural, social-emotional and learning needs:** Being cognizant of individuals' backgrounds and needs (e.g. accessibility, language, personal) as well as group dynamics (e.g. setting norms, etc.).

4. **Facilitating active learning:** Leading professional learning that engages educators in authentic or simulated activities, such as design challenges, problems of practice and reflection.

5. **Meaningful feedback:** Feedback that is specific, actionable and results in improvements or changes to practice.

6. **Evaluate the impact of professional learning:** Measuring and analyzing participant feedback about specific professional learning, and evaluating aggregated professional learning against system goals for changes in culture or teacher practice.

A systematic process is developed as the coach carefully and thoughtfully plans, executes and evaluates professional learning at the districtwide or schoolwide level, and at the individual educator and leader levels. Planning begins with a needs assessment on what students are doing well in the school and individual classes, as well as what can be improved. The educational needs of school educators and leaders are examined at the whole-school level, and also for the needs of each individual adult, to consider their pre-existing skills, knowledge and confidence with technology to then move forward with a plan.

Learning happens in a nonjudgmental fashion via a method based on understanding how the brain works from the learning sciences, and takes into account learner preference. The coach supports all learners by using well-developed frameworks, such as the ISTE Standards for Students, ISTE Standards for Educators and ISTE Standards for Education Leaders. Effective coaches introduce the ISTE Standards and other strategies with active, empowering learning experiences for educators and leaders with purposeful, useful feedback. Effective coaches understand that evaluation needs to be planned and executed on a regular basis as learner needs change and evolve.

 Great facilitation is the art of assisting discovery.

There are three indicators to accompany this standard. The first has coaches designing professional learning with a strong foundation of needs assessment data and adult learning frameworks. The second indicator highlights capacity-building of educators, leaders and instructional teams by using the ISTE Standards as a road map. Learning is an active, hands-on, empowering experience with the coach providing supportive, clear and purposeful feedback to the adult learners. The final indicator emphasizes that evaluation is key to understanding the change that's needed and the future directions to ensure technology provides high-impact teaching and learning.

Here are examples of how ISTE members connect with this standard:

> The trick with professional development is to meet teachers where they are, without judgment. Sometimes that means a private way of "catching up." To help teachers feel comfortable with little things, I started the Tissue Tabloid (#PottyPD) with a math teacher. We share bite-size information on a sheet that hangs in the bathroom. The information includes simple things like how to pin a tab in Chrome to the routine like how to change your password to the complex like where to go to get more information. We also added a mini literacy lesson and cartoons to bring humor and the culture together. #PottyPD has been a great success for helping teachers move forward without making them feel uncomfortable.
>
> — Robbie Barber, Georgia

> The educators in my building have varying schedules and differing needs, so I've designed and continued to iterate upon a multifaceted professional learning model. I hold whole-school PD sessions on a quarterly basis and I hold tech workshops every Tuesday, right after school. This type of learning doesn't work for everyone though! Because of this, I've also started a weekly podcast that our educators can listen to on their commutes and a blog they can read in their spare time. I have also designed professional learning courses on a Teachable site that our educators can access on demand. All of these components come together in a way that meets the needs of all of our teacher learners and helps to build capacity when they feel ready in the areas they can identify as needs for themselves.
>
> — Nicole Welsh, Washington, D.C.

6. Data-Driven Decision-Maker

Coaches model and support the use of qualitative and quantitative data to inform their own instruction and professional learning. Coaches:

a. Assist educators and leaders[1] in securely collecting and analyzing student data[2].

b. Support educators to interpret qualitative and quantitative data to inform their decisions[3] and support individual student learning.

c. Partner with educators to empower students to use learning data[4] to set their own goals and measure their progress.

There's no question that instructional technology coaches work hard to promote effective technology use in schools. However, effective coaches pinpoint their direction of effort. In a backward-design approach, coaches think about the learning goal and discern which, if any, technology would deepen student learning. Careful thought is then given to the types of data that will determine how and if that goal is being achieved. Quantitative data is collected, such as individual, school and district test scores, that provide information on whether a strategy or initiative was effective. Qualitative data, such as observation notes and student work samples, provide data on *how* and *why* an initiative was effective. Together, these types of data provide important information that informs coaches about what's been effective in the past and what needs improving to move the school forward to high-impact technology use. Effective coaches use their expertise to mentor educators and leaders on how to collect and analyze data, while modeling safe digital data management that complies with data privacy, confidentiality and security practices.

---

1. **Educators and leaders:** Includes education stakeholders (e.g. classroom teachers, principals, instructional leaders, district leaders and administrators, (policymakers), as appropriate.

2. **Securely collecting and analyzing student data:** Practices that protect information and data through precautionary planning and actions, such as training to establish and maintain best practices among educators, complying with state and federal regulations for protecting student data and privacy, and choosing technology products and solution providers that have robust privacy policies and security capabilities.

3. **Interpret qualitative and quantitative data to inform decisions:** Ability to evaluate methodological (e.g. surveys, observations, etc.) and statistical data, determine course of action based on data and take action, such as instructional modifications, groupings, personalizing or accommodating student needs.

4. **Learning data:** A wide variety of data sources regarding students, such as academic data that supports planning and goal setting, formative and summative assessments, attendance, etc.

Coaches work with educators in collecting, analyzing and interpreting the data. Research shows that educators often don't know how to use data effectively to improve student learning outcomes (Mandinach & Gummer, 2016). Coaches empower educators to skillfully use data as a powerful tool that informs teaching and learning by looking at class trends, such as if the class as a whole is struggling with a concept, or tracking individual students who may have errors or misconceptions on a number of questions related to a particular concept.

Effective coaches also bring in students to develop a growth mindset through creating individualized goals and promoting skills that lead to lifelong learners.

 Old ways keep doors closed to improvement. Data-driven decisions ensure the right doors are opened to lead learners in the right direction.

There are four indicators to accompany this standard. The first indicator emphasizes student data privacy, something required by law and that should be routine practice. The second indicator is vital because it helps us, as coaches and educators, understand and use data to adapt instruction to meet student needs. The final indicator supports the shift in both the educator and student roles, whereby educators empower students and students become agents of their own data and learning. Student involvement is key to a shared vision of learning goals and understanding of future learning pathways.

Here are examples of how ISTE members connect with this standard:

> We're in our second year of implementing an initiative – a growth assessment for literacy and math. As a coach, it's my responsibility to support the teachers in using this assessment tool. Students take the assessment three times a year and teachers then have detailed data to drive their classroom instruction. Along with our literacy and math coaches, we guide the teachers in understanding how to read the data, group students and inform their instructional practices. Understanding of the data, the program and the additional applications for students is my part in ensuring the professional development and technology supports teachers in meeting the needs of the students.
>
> — Dawn Jones, Florida

> As someone who coaches teachers and school leadership on how to best leverage technology to support teaching and learning, collecting and analyzing student data to support decision-making is a constant process. In working with teachers directly, data is the first step we review together. It involves looking at several sources of student achievement data to help us better triangulate the instructional focus and, most importantly, the impact we aim to have on individual student learning.
>
> — James Centeno, California

7. Digital Citizen Advocate

Coaches model digital citizenship and support educators and students in recognizing the responsibilities and opportunities inherent in living in a digital world. Coaches:

a. Inspire and encourage educators and students to use technology for civic engagement[1] and to address challenges to improve their communities.

b. Partner with educators, leaders, students and families to foster a culture of respectful online interactions[2] and a healthy balance in their use of technology[3].

c. Support educators and students to critically examine the sources of online media[4] and identify underlying assumptions[5].

d. Empower educators, leaders and students to make informed decisions to protect their personal data[6] and curate the digital profile they intend to reflect[7].

Digital citizenship is more than student safety that was highlighted in the early years of internet use. Stories of fear and avoidance are now replaced with opportunities for students to be the change they want to see in the world. As today's students are immersed in a digital world, effective coaches model and advocate for digital citizenship best practices that involve educators and students recognizing citizenship responsibilities. Effective coaches model and support educators and students in recognizing how the internet can be used for civic engagement and to actively improve the local, state and national physical and online community. Students benefit from active participation and awareness of their local communities. Coaches promote student and educator understanding that the online space is also a community of people with rights and responsibilities.

---

1. **Use technology for civic engagement:** Becoming an informed citizen and making positive and socially responsible contributions, such as crowdfunding for a cause or mobilizing others to participate in a cause, vote and volunteer.

2. **Culture of respectful online interactions:** Creating shared values for civil, inclusive and humane online interactions and communication, such as standing up for others online and being empathetic and aware of others' perspectives and experiences.

3. **Healthy balance in their use of technology:** Maintaining positive self-esteem when using social media and self-regulating time online to ensure well-being and physical health.

4. **Critically examine the sources of online media:** Ability to evaluate the credibility, accuracy and relevance of data, multimedia and online sources.

5. **Underlying assumptions:** Ability to recognize the perspective of an author and purpose or bias of information sources.

6. **Informed decisions to protect their personal data:** Understands how networked devices (e.g., phones, smart devices) and online sites collect user information and implement settings that control levels of data that an individual wants to share.

7. **Curate the digital profile they intend to reflect:** Ability to represent oneself online based on activities and connections or tagging through social media posts, photos, public online comments or reviews.

Coaches advocate for positive citizenship to be modeled on the broader scale as they work with educators, leaders, students and families to develop a respectful online community and healthy, positive technology use. Coaches advocate for positive online behaviors as well as a healthy balance of technology use for physical and mental well-being. Coaches work to ensure all parties are critical consumers of internet content and have strategies and techniques to validate websites and content.

A critical part of the coach's role in digital citizenship is to ensure students, teachers and leaders have the knowledge and understanding of how each person's digital footprint is developed, and the importance of developing a digital footprint that represents the image that person wishes to reflect now and in the future. A digital footprint is developed from a person's trail they've left on the internet. It's the content posted by the user, including text, images, video posts, "likes" and comments on social media and emails sent. It's also the passive digital content, such as websites visited and information submitted to online services. Despite the emphasis on positive digital footprints as students go forward to college and job applications, in-the-moment actions can often lead to regrets. Coaches work with educators, leaders and students to make informed decisions to protect their personal data and curate the digital profile they intend to reflect.

 We are all digital citizens. We just need to be sure that we are responsible digital citizens.

There are four indicators to accompany this standard. The first highlights the positive use of technology for civic engagement and work toward improving the communities, both digital and physical, that the educator and students live in. The second indicator has the coach partnering with those in and out of school to promote respectful online interactions. It also includes coaches advocating for a healthy balance of technology use for positive physical and cognitive well-being. The third indicator supports educators and students in being critical consumers of online content. The final indicator is focused on digital footprints and data as coaches empower educators, leaders and students to make informed, positive decisions on the data they provide on the web and the digital profile they wish to reflect.

Here are examples of how ISTE members connect with this standard:

> As our middle schools move to 1:1 devices, we've been working with administration teams to develop plans for implementation. These plans focus on logistics, but also more broadly on developing schoolwide culture surrounding digital citizenship. Specifically, with one middle school, I've developed a rollout plan that includes student assemblies, crowdsourcing teachers for best practices, and teacher training surrounding thoughtful technology integration and digital citizenship. We're working with the administration to prepare teachers to be model digital citizens who use technology to improve instruction in a global society.
>
> — Annie Cohn, Massachusetts

> Digital citizenship is about developing and promoting committed and interested citizens who use technology for their good, for their well-being and for that of their community as indicated by the standard. If we delve into its indicators, the one that presents us with the greatest challenges is "inspiring and encouraging educators and students to use technology for civic engagement." Make it clear that, today, being a citizen is being a digital citizen.
>
> — Cristina Escobar, Chile

Coaching and the ISTE Standards

The coach has to ensure a great many pieces of the puzzle are in place to see the big picture of high-impact teaching and learning with digital technology. There may seem like many pieces scattered in different directions and working independently, but effective coaches bring these pieces together to have them working effectively. These standards can be used by coaches to guide their professional growth plans or by human resources staff to develop job descriptions or interview questions. ISTE has used research-based best practices, information from the learning sciences and a vast number of educational stakeholders to confirm that these standards are valuable instruments in the coach's toolbox.

The ISTE Standards provide a role-based set of skills that students, educators, education leaders and coaches need. The standards define success in using technology to teach, lead or coach.

While defined by role, the standards are nested, with educators using the Educator Standards and Student Standards, and leaders using the Education Leader Standards, Educator Standards and Student Standards. An effective coach uses the family of standards in their role at the school or district to empower all people in education to use technology effectively. See Figure 2.

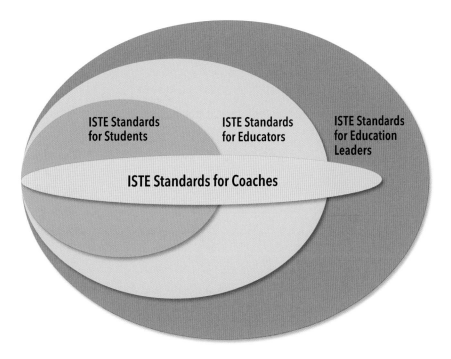

Figure 2. Coaches bridge the three sets of standards integrating and moving between them.

ISTE Standards for Students

Students are at the heart of everything we do. At the ground level, the ISTE Standards for Students (2016) explain what students can do to optimize their learning with digital technologies. They're designed to empower student voice and ensure that learning is a student-driven process. These standards leverage positive teaching and learning practices with technology to promote the development of student attributes to ensure learning, with the goal of cultivating these skills onward throughout a student's academic career and beyond. There are seven student standards: Empowered Learner, Digital Citizen, Knowledge Constructor, Innovative Designer, Computational Thinker, Creative Communicator and Global Collaborator.

Students are *empowered learners* who set goals, build networks, troubleshoot and transfer knowledge to new situations. Students are *digital citizens* who cultivate a positive digital identity, modeling positive, safe, legal and ethical online behaviors. Students are *knowledge constructors* who employ research strategies to find resources and information; evaluate the accuracy, credibility and relevance of information; and build knowledge through exploring real-world issues and problems. Students are *innovative designers* who use a design process for generating ideas, testing theories and creating knowledge and innovative artifacts; select and use digital tools to plan and manage design processes; develop, test and refine prototypes; and exhibit tolerance for ambiguity and perseverance with open-ended problems.

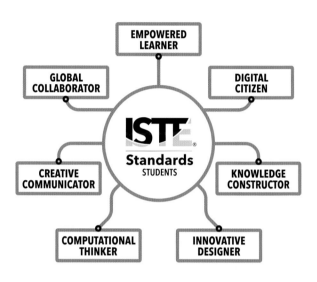

Students are *computational thinkers* who collect, select and analyze data, and use technology for data analysis, abstract models and algorithmic thinking. Students are *creative communicators* who choose appropriate platforms and tools for creation or communication; communicate ideas using a variety of digital objects, such as visualizations, models or simulations; and present customized messages and mediums for various audiences. Finally, students are *global collaborators* who broaden their perspectives and enrich their learning by collaborating with others and working effectively in teams locally and globally.

Explore the ISTE Standards for Students

iste.org/standards/for-students

Coaches use the Student Standards as a benchmark of skills that students build over their academic careers, so when they graduate they have demonstrated competency in them. Coaches also support students by ensuring that digital tools and programs are available to meet learning goals and the diverse needs of students, including grade, preference, gender, culture, race, physical and emotional, and cognitive abilities.

The master coach embodies the characteristics found in the ISTE Standards for Students, such as being *innovative designers* and *knowledge constructors*, while supporting students in becoming Creative Communicators as they work with peers and the larger community.

ISTE Standards for Educators

The ISTE Standards for Educators (2017) embrace the shift from teacher-driven to student-driven learning. These standards provide pathways for educators to leverage technology to transform teaching and learning. They also show educators learning alongside their students and educators leading others locally and globally. There are seven educator standards: Learner, Leader, Citizen, Collaborator, Designer, Facilitator and Analyst.

Educators are *learners* who set goals, pursue professional interests and stay current with research. Educators are *leaders* who shape, advance and accelerate a shared vision of empowered learning with technology, advocate for equitable access and model good practices for colleagues. Educators are *citizens* who engage and focus their students in contributing and participating in the digital world through creating experiences, establishing a learning culture and mentoring students in safe, legal and ethical practices. Educators are *collaborators* who commit time to working with colleagues and students, demonstrating cultural competency and using digital technology in collaborative efforts.

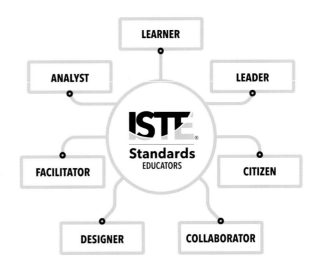

Educators are *designers* who use technology to personalize learning experiences, design authentic learning activities and apply instructional design principles. Educators are *facilitators* who match learning that has students reflect the characteristics in the ISTE Standards for Students by developing a culture of ownership, managing digital learning strategies and modeling creativity and expression. Educators are *analysts* who use data to drive instruction with a variety of assessment practices that accommodate for learner needs, provide timely feedback and communicate with all educational stakeholders.

Explore the ISTE Standards for Educators

iste.org/standards-for-educators

Coaches support educators to meet their individual professional goals for using technology and work with educators to ensure that the ISTE Standards for Students are met.

Effective coaches are key in supporting professional development; they work with educators to set learning goals; empower educators to model best practices for peers; advocate for equal access for all students; and prepare educators to design and facilitate instructional technology best practices while using data to drive decision-making. Coaches provide modeling, collaborative learning and facilitation through iterative methodologies to support educators in meeting those goals.

ISTE Standards for Education Leaders

The ISTE Standards for Education Leaders reflect the shift from manager to facilitator who leverages digital technologies to build a positive learning landscape in their classroom, school, district and beyond. These standards highlight how to develop a system that embraces shared leadership, trust and encouragement. There are five educational leader standards: Equity and Citizenship Advocate, Visionary Planner, Empowering Leader, Systems Designer and Connected Learner.

Education leaders are *equity and citizenship advocates* as they ensure all students have skilled teachers, all students have access to technology for authentic/ engaging learning opportunities and critically evaluate online resources while cultivating safe, ethical and legal use of technology. Education leaders are *visionary planners* as they develop and adopt a shared vision and strategic plan for technology use with an ongoing cycle of evaluation and share what they have learned with others. Educational leaders are *empowering leaders* who empower and build competency of educators while inspiring a culture of innovation and meeting the needs of all learners.

Education leaders are *systems designers* who establish robust infrastructure and systems, ensure sufficient and scalable resources, and protect the privacy and security with data management policies. Finally, education leaders are *connected learners* who regularly take part in professional learning practices, remain current with emerging technologies and develop skills to advance systems and promote continuous improvement.

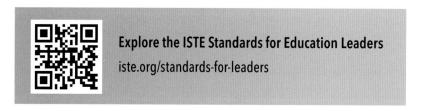

Explore the ISTE Standards for Education Leaders

iste.org/standards-for-leaders

Coaches support educators to meet their individual professional goals for using technology and work with educators to ensure that the ISTE Standards for students are met.

Effective coaches are key in supporting professional development as effective coaches work with educators to set learning goals, empower educators to model best practices for peers, advocate for equal access for all students, and prepare educators to design, facilitate instructional technology best-practices while using data to drive that decision making. Coaches provide modeling, collaborative learning, facilitation through iterative methodologies to support educators in meeting those goals.

Coaching Methodologies

The overarching goal of an instructional technology coach is to improve teaching and learning with technology. This is a task that involves a complex interconnected relationship with people, digital technology and systems. While a coach with great passion may want to run at the task and tackle each need and challenge as it arises, this is often not an effective method of coaching. Instead, effective coaches work using a carefully planned strategic methodology based on the learning sciences and developed to achieve high-impact use of technology. Strong methodologies provide clarity to your task of extending and enhancing educator and leader skill sets.

There are various types of strategies for coaches to use. Past practices often had coaches implementing an initiative or providing one- or two-day training on tool use. Research shows that this "one-and-done" method of coaching is ineffective and that repeated, iterative support is needed (Crompton, Olszewski & Bielefeldt, 2016). The learning sciences also provide a host of information as to how people learn and adopt new strategies and tools. Based on information from research and the learning sciences, various types of coaching cycles have emerged.

Coaching Cycles

Coaching cycles are cyclical frameworks put in place by the coach to ensure those educators and educational leaders who they serve are improving systems and practices. Coaching cycles include a set of purposeful steps that are repeated to continue the cycle of improvement. There are various types of coaching cycles and they should be selected based on what works best for those in the coaching context. Coaches can even select pieces of different coaching cycles or use multiple cycles at the same time. It's important the chosen cycle is agreed upon by those whom the coach is working with. In this section, various coaching cycles for working with educators and education leaders are explained.

Coaching cycles are a set of purposeful steps that are repeated to continue the cycle of improvement.

Types of Coaching Cycles

The first choice in selecting a coaching cycle is to determine if cycles will be implemented one-on-one or as a group. You may want to do both, depending on educator needs.

One-on-One Coaching Cycle	Group Coaching Cycle
In-depth, focused work with an individual educator.	Group work with educators who share a common goal or set of goals.
Focused on a goal identified through self-selection or student data.	Focused on a goal identified through self-selection, student data or a larger schoolwide or district initiative.
Involves a specific number of times each week in the classroom for modeling, teaching, and strategic observation.	Involves group conversations that can also include coach and peer modeling, and feedback in class.

Example Coaching Cycles

Each of these cycles are described for one-on-one coaching scenarios. However, they can also be modified for group coaching. Furthermore, the authors typically describe the cycles while focusing on the educator. Aligned to the ISTE Standards for Coaches, effective coaches work with educators and education leaders. These methodologies can be used to work with all who are working toward improved practices.

Expeditionary Learning Education Coaching Cycle

In this EL Education (2015) coaching cycle, there are four parts: Goal-setting, learning, observation and data collection, and reflection (See Figure 3). What's interesting about this coaching cycle is that it highlights data collection as one of the key tasks. This is a crucial aspect in really understanding if a strategy and/or technology is working or not. Cycles can often run on perceptions of the educator and coach that are not always accurate. This step has the educator and coach really digging in to look at other data to investigate with more focused evidence.

Figure 3. Coaching cycle (EL Education, 2015).

Goal-setting is at the core of this coaching cycle and is what guides the coaching relationship. The goals are based on the individual goals of the educator and the larger school improvement priorities. The "learning phase" is through "school-based professional development, institutes and practices, such as looking at student work; reading and discussing educational texts; observing best practices (e.g. model teaching, peer observation, use of video), co-teaching; and collaborative planning of curriculum, instruction and assessment" (EL Education, 2015).

Authors of this coaching cycle also remind coaches that educators don't necessarily start at goal-setting and may start at other points in the cycle.

Knight Impact Cycle

Knight (2018) designed the Impact Cycle made up of three iterating phases: identify, learn and improve (See Figure 4). This methodology is detailed and has multiple checklists and question banks to be used at each of those phases. In the *identify* phase, the main activity is for the educator and coach to watch a video of the educator working with students. Before the video recording, there's a pre-observation checklist that the coach uses to make sure that they gather the information they need from the video. This includes basic logistics, such as date, time, lesson, where the coach will be in the classroom during the video recording and, most importantly, what the educator would like the coach to focus on for development.

The coach and educator then watch the video together and the coach asks a set of "identify questions" that help focus the conversation. Then the educator identifies a student-focused goal.

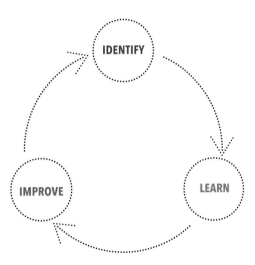

Figure 4. The Impact Cycle (Knight, 2018).

The next phase of Knight's model is the *learn* phase. This begins with the coach sharing a checklist for the educator's chosen strategies of focus. The coach prompts the educator to modify their existing practice. The educator then chooses an approach to modeling they would like to observe and the coach does the modeling. The educator then schedules a time they will practice what they've observed. The final phase, *improve*, has the educator practicing what they have learned with the coach observing in class or from a video taken by the educator. During the practice, the coach collects data on the activities of the educator or on the students as related to the goal from the identify phase. The educator and coach review the data and, from further discussion, make adaptations to practice and plan next steps until the goal is met.

The Professional Institute of Instructional Coaching 3-Step Cycle

Similar to Knight, the Professional Institute (2017) advocates for a three-step, *before, during and after* cycle of consultation. This is similar to Knight's framework, but simplified in language and activities. This may work for a coach who is new to coaching cycles as it's easy to follow. Knight's framework may be best for someone who wants more specific details and supporting frameworks, such as sets of questions and checklists to ask in the various phases. For the institute's coaching cycle, in the *before* step, the coach works with the educator to co-construct the goals for the cycle. In the *during* step, the coach provides support and the educator takes steps toward that goal with the coach present. The *after* cycle is when the coach and educator deconstruct what happened toward the goal with a discussion on what happened and what steps to take to improvement.

Corwin Coaching Cycle

The Corwin Coaching Cycle has six phases:

1. Set standards-based goals
2. Develop targets
3. Pre-assess
4. Co-plan
5. Co-teach
6. Post-assess

This coaching cycle is similar in nature to the other frameworks listed. Phase one reminds users to set goals based on standards to move student learning forward as they note that growth cannot be measured without these goals. In phase two, the coach works with the educator to develop targets that are a breakdown of the goal in phase one. This is to provide a vision and criteria for what students will need to know and do to meet that target. The pre-assess phase is a little different than other coaching cycles as it requires a baseline of student proficiency based on a formative assessment. In phases four and five, the coach and educator work collaboratively to co-plan and co-teach. The final phase of Corwin's cycle is to conduct a post-assessment to measure student progress toward learning. This will then be used to determine next steps to continue the iterative cycle of improvement.

This coaching cycle is similar in nature to the other frameworks listed. Phase one reminds users to set goals based on standards to move student learning forward as they note that growth cannot be measured without these goals. In phase two, the coach works with the educator to develop targets that are a breakdown of the goal in phase one. This is to provide a vision and criteria for what students will need to know and do to meet that target. The pre-assess phase is a little different than other coaching cycles as it requires a baseline of student proficiency based on a formative assessment. In phases four and five, the coach and educator work collaboratively to co-plan and co-teach. The final phase of Corwin's cycle is to conduct a post-assessment to measure student progress toward learning. This will then be used to determine next steps to continue the iterative cycle of improvement.

Coaching Vignettes

These vignettes show examples from a diverse range of schools: rural to urban; technology-strong to starting with technology; public, diocese and independent schools; and large and small schools. These coaches embody the ISTE Standards for Coaches as they straddle the on-the-ground and leadership vision.

Change Agent

Holly Miller and Kevin Anderle

Holly Miller and Kevin Anderle are instructional technology specialists at Garfield County Schools in Rifle, Colorado. This is a rural district with six elementary schools, two middle schools and two high schools. This district serves 4,789 students with 52% minority students and 45% receiving free and reduced-price lunch. To connect leaders and educators to maximize the potential of technology in the district, Miller and Anderle are in the process of supporting a district implementation of a WHHW (What, How, How, What) Coaching Cycle.

Within this framework, teachers plan what they teach within the state standards (W), how to best teach that content (H), and how to assess what has been taught (H). Teachers also plan what to do if students already understand a topic or if students did not master the content that was taught (W). These coaches recognize educators across the district who use technology effectively to enable high-impact teaching and learning, and use them as exemplars in the process.

> We have a compass that's the umbrella for everything WHHW, and transcendent technology is the needle in the middle of the compass.
>
> — Holly Miller and Kevin Anderle, Instructional Technology Specialists

Working with leaders is also important, and Anderle and Miller have developed training for the superintendent and assistant superintendent of the district, as well as the curriculum director and director of technology so they could gain a "conversational understanding" of digital frameworks. After several training sessions with district administration, they describe a shared vision across the district on the effective use of technology that highly impacts teaching and learning. They share their next steps in working with principals and then building-level academic coaches at an even deeper level to help teachers with the integration during coaching cycles and unit planning.

Miller and Anderle are change agents who recognize the different needs of all learners, working with both educators and educational leaders with these initiatives to accelerate transformation.

Irene Orozco

Irene Orozco is an informational technology program specialist at ABC Unified School District in Cerritos, California. ABC Unified is an urban district southeast of Los Angeles and serves a TK–12 student population of 20,137 students. This is an ethnically diverse population with over 7,000 English language learners. Orozco tries hard to be a change agent in her school district, working closely to coach both educators and educational leaders to support all learners with high-impact technology use.

An important part of this standard for Orozco is cultivating a supportive coaching culture that encourages educators and leaders to achieve a shared vision and individual goals with equitable access to learning for all. At ABC Unified, she offers self-selected options for professional learning to meet educator and leader needs through intentional and strategic digital learning that recognizes, validates and meets the level, interest and needs of educators.

> My goal is for all teachers to use grade-appropriate technology tools to teach and build their skills for the classroom and beyond. Critical to the success of this goal is the supportive culture for teachers during the implementation phases and incremental steps toward their learning outcomes.
>
> — Irene Orozco, IT Program Specialist

Orozco recognizes educators across the organization who use technology effectively to enable positive technology use in the classroom and school. She built a sharing, connected culture by having educators share lesson ideas, look at student work and observe their colleagues. They exchange ideas for innovation and creativity in their lessons and talk about effective technology integration in core curricular areas. Orozco has found that as educators visited other classrooms, they became more willing to take risks and experiment with new ways to work with technology to enhance their lessons.

> At the heart of our programs is the idea that we're all learners and we can move forward together. I focus on being a change agent who's instrumental in supporting and encouraging change and modelling flexibility, diverse skills, commitment to the shared vision and the willingness to change my own instructional practice and share that with others, enabling many teachers to do the same.
>
> — Irene Orozco, IT Program Specialist

Connected Learner

Carolina Seiden

Carolina Seiden is an academic technologist at Saint Andrew's School in Florida, a suburban school serving 1,300 students. Seiden works with a group of others in academic technology who actively engage in learning experiences to extend and enhance their knowledge, skills and behaviors with technology.

This team is currently working on their individual portfolios for ISTE Certification for Educators. They're supporting each other in gaining a better understanding of the ISTE Standards for Educators so they can support the educators at Saint Andrews. Seiden and her group also are reading books together, including the ISTE book *Teach Boldly: Edtech for Social Good* by Jennifer Williams.

> What is the point of all of the frameworks, data analysis, pedagogical debates and curricular alignment without coming together to be a force of good?
>
> — Carolina Seiden, Academic Technologist

For Seiden, it's the shared vision of our community that guides her work, projects and to-do lists. The school's vision for technology is clearly articulated. The action steps are measurable, the direction clear, and Seiden and the team proudly follow, lead and support these altruistic pursuits.

Transitioning from full-time teaching to coaching has given me a lifelong lesson: You either get bitter or you get better. When I'm collaborating with a colleague or a group of them, the feedback is instantaneous and the only way to respond to it is to grow, to get better at listening, reaching out, understanding the needs and encouraging my colleagues to see in themselves what I see. I will forever treasure this opportunity to find MY better.

— Carolina Seiden, Academic Technologist

Wanda Terral

Wanda Terral is a director of technology at Lakeland School District in Tennessee, a two-school rural district. Terral spent 13 years as an educational technology coach, and her current role has her working closely with technology facilitators at Lakeland School System. She's able to share the knowledge she gained from the years of experience in educational technology. Terral embodies the Connected Learner standard as she seeks out multiple ways to be connected and learn from and with others.

For me, #BetterTogether is not just a hashtag — it's a call to action. It's an acknowledgment that I must be open to learning from others and that I have a duty to contribute to the conversation. I made a Twitter account in December of 2009 but didn't utilize it as a PLN for another three years. I began as a lurker, consuming goodness shared by others, but evolved into sharing my own insights and resources. I was giddy the first time someone retweeted me, thrilled I'd shared something that was useful to someone else. It became a personal goal to share and help even more people. I've had the honor of meeting many of my tweeps face to face and thanking them for helping me grow my skills over the years. By actively participating in my PLN I'm able to enhance my coaching practice and keep current with emerging technology and innovations in pedagogy and the learning sciences. That PLN also provides me with the opportunity to give back to those who have given me so much over the years. #BetterTogether!"

— Wanda Terral, Director of Technology

Collaborator

Lisa Kuhn

Lisa Kuhn is an educational technology integration specialist at Forward Edge and a technology coach at Little Miami School District Maineville and Morrow in Ohio. This is a rural district with over 4,500 students. Her role is to work with all educators across the K–12 district. She started this role by making it clear she wanted her work to be a collaborative partnership and dove in by consulting with a district of 250+ teachers in six different buildings, grades PK–12, four days a week. She took time to investigate the wants and needs of those in the district.

Kuhn is a strong advocate for collaboration and she exemplifies this in her coaching cycles with educators at the schools. In her coaching cycles, she uses a version of backward design. As a partner with educators, Kuhn works with educators to set goals, brainstorm ideas for activities and tools, plan and prepare lessons, implement lessons (via co-teaching, solo teaching with coaching and observation, or the coach modeling teaching the lesson), and reflect on the result.

Ultimately, the coaching cycle is a great way to grow relationships as teacher and coach explore together, brainstorm together and learn to trust each other as they discover new or modified ways of engaging students in their learning. I find that I learn as much (or more) from my teachers as they learn from me and I love that part!

— Lisa Kuhn, Educational Technology Integration Specialist/Technology Coach

Kuhn worked closely with an educator in the school to explore new instructional strategies and identify learning content and tools, and then together they planned for the effective use of technology.

In the coaching cycle for an eighth grade art teacher, we discussed an upcoming lesson (Impressionism). First, we looked at goals/the final project product and used backward design to develop the lesson which we co-taught. The final product ended up being a "pop-impressionism" project where students reproduced a painting from either the impressionist or post-impressionist period and included an animated character in the final 'painting.' The teacher and I discussed the background information needed so students could better understand the history of impressionism and the concept of blending it with pop culture. From there, we collaborated on the resources and the steps in the project.

— Lisa Kuhn, Educational Technology Integration Specialist/Technology Coach

Keith Hannah

Keith Hannah is a district instructional technology facilitator at Fife Public Schools in Fife, Washington. This suburban school district serves approximately 3,500 students. Hannah is a role model and advocate for establishing productive relationships with educators to improve instructional practice and learning outcomes.

Recently, Hannah introduced virtual reality (VR) to the teachers he works with. Many of the educators were excited, but some were hesitant, wondering about how to manage the hardware/software side. Hannah offered to work with educators individually in their classrooms.

I always extend an invitation to come to their classroom to be a source of support and assistance as they're trying something new with edtech. Not every teacher needs this level of support, but I do find some of our teachers really want that extra safety net when taking a foray into the unknown. A "we're trying this together" approach really fosters trust between teachers and myself as an instructional coach.

— Keith Hannah, District Instructional Technology Facilitator

Hannah also worked to build partnerships with groups of educators (individual groups such as the social studies teachers) to select VR experiences that matched the content.

With my support, the teachers could focus on delivering the content of the expedition and not have to be so fearful of what might happen if things didn't go as planned. My favorite quote of the day was a student who exclaimed, "This is WAY better than field trips! Let's do more of this from now on!" This happened through the teacher and I collaborating together.

— Keith Hannah, District Instructional Technology Facilitator

Learning Designer

Dominic Caguioa

Dominic Caguioa is a coordinator of instructional leadership support as part of the Instructional Technology Initiative in the Los Angeles Unified School District (LAUSD), an urban school district serving approximately 600,000 students. Caguioa focuses his attention on effective instructional design.

> I maintain the mindset of "leading with instruction" consistent with our department's mission to put learning first, technology second.
>
> — Dominic Caguioa, Coordinator of Instructional Leadership Support/Instructional Technology Initiative

Caguioa models and supports educators in designing learning experiences and environments to meet the needs of all students by using the suite of ISTE Standards. In LAUSD, the focus is the application of a "Triple Track Approach" where educators can a) Learn for themselves during these sessions; b) Learn how they might get other adults to learn the same thing they're learning; and c) Learn how they might apply this learning in their classroom for student learning. Coaching and professional learning at LAUSD exemplifies the implementation of the ISTE Standards, following the Triple Track Approach. Adapted from the Thinking Collaborative's Adaptive Schools, LAUSD designs professional learning by intentionally considering:

- Track 1 is the individual's learning of content and strategies with the lens of the ISTE Standards for Educators, really looking at how coaching and PD strategies might support educators and leaders in their own learning.

- Track 2 is taking into account that the educators they coach and provide PD forgo back to their school sites and share their learning with their peers and colleagues, so they embed the ISTE Standards for Education Leaders as these participants go on to facilitate the learning of other educators.

- Track 3 is to ensure that they always put students at the center of coaching and professional learning. Using the Student Standards, the sessions ensure that there are opportunities for participants to engage in lesson design, delivery, feedback and reflection.

> As a coach working at the systems level, it's important to approach the work in a holistic way in order to not lose sight of our end goal of student learning. This is where the Triple Track Approach to the implementation of the ISTE Standards works seamlessly in ensuring that while my main charge is to design and support professional learning for a system as large as L.A. Unified, I also need to think about the teachers in the classroom and how they, as adult learners, also need to learn effectively for themselves first in order to trickle, or better yet, cascade the learning down to the very students they serve in their classrooms.
>
> — Dominic Caguioa, Coordinator of Instructional Leadership Support/Instructional Technology Initiative

Mary Norris

Mary Norris is an instructional technology coach at Achievable Dream Middle and High School in Newport News, Virginia. This is an urban school serving approximately 420 underserved students with 100% receiving free or reduced-price lunch, 88% African American, 9% Hispanic and 3% caucasian/other. Norris was part of a team that sought out strategies for a more effective coaching approach with teachers. Personalized learning opportunities were a major focus in this endeavor, along with a drive toward authentic, active learning experiences that foster student agency, deepen content mastery and allow students to demonstrate their competency.

An example of Norris' efforts included partnering with a sixth grade English teacher to highlight personalized learning opportunities in the classroom and provide concrete examples. She built a strong partnership with the English teacher that began with an initial extensive discussion about the teacher's goals and connecting technologies.

> We discussed various ways that students could demonstrate learning and gave careful consideration to curriculum, the ISTE Standards and what level of SAMR is demonstrated upon completion of an assignment. We didn't want to integrate technology just because students had continued access to technology, but because we wanted to make each use meaningful and enable students to demonstrate competency in various ways.
>
> — Mary Norris, Instructional Technology Coach

As they work together, Norris values the teacher's curriculum content expertise and ensures technological fit with specific questions to the teacher. She then models for the teacher and students the effective use of technology in the classroom and demonstrates of how various programs could be used to accomplish their assignments, providing vivid examples along the way. Reflection was a very important part of this partnership, with discussions reflecting back to the initial goals and improvements going forward.

Professional Learning Facilitator

Gregory Gilmore

Gregory is an educational technology coach at Osage Trail Middle School in Independence, Missouri. The Fort Osage R–1 school district serves approximately 5,000 students in rural to urban areas. Gregory works in a close team with two other coaches with a shared vision and philosophy to empower leaders, educators and students with technology. This team spirit is reflected in practice at the school. Gregory works with educators to conduct needs assessments to ensure he's meeting their cultural, social-emotional and learning needs.

Gregory facilitates instructional rounds that allow teachers to visit classrooms and then reflect on those visits as a collaborative team. Instructional rounds are used as a protocol for in-house professional learning and focused on a problem of practice that could be observed within the instructional core. The coaches set a rounds schedule for the day, prebrief with the visiting teachers beforehand, observe classrooms together, reflect on that visit as a team, and then set personal goals based on classroom visits and conversations of the day. As the faculty became more comfortable visiting each other's classrooms, they began setting goals as a content team and then customizing their professional development around those goals and holding each other accountable as they worked toward those goals.

This coaching cycle/instructional rounds are an important part of facilitation at Osage Trail Middle School. Each cycle of instructional rounds was organized differently to meet the needs of the staff and provide them the opportunities they needed to grow. The process involves three steps:

1. Prebrief, establishing norms and procedures.

2. Observation, classroom visits.

3. Debrief, reflection and goal-setting.

> Our primary goals for facilitating instructional rounds focus on creating a culture that supports collaborative learning to meet the current needs of individual teachers and professional learning communities. Through gradually releasing the responsibility of planning instructional rounds cycles to individual professional learning communities, we allowed teachers to take ownership of their professional development, giving them the opportunity to learn from each other and work together to improve instruction and student learning. Over time, we saw teachers build capacity in instructional effectiveness and peer leadership, which further strengthened the culture of collaborative and personalized learning.
>
> — Gregory Gilmore, Educational Technology Coach

Cammie Kannekens

Cammie Kannekens is an instructional coach at Prairie Rose School Division No.8 in Alberta, Canada. This is a rural school district serving approximately 2,500 students in 19 schools. The district includes a number of very small schools, such as K–9 schools with 30 students and K–5 schools with 12 students. Technology is a valuable tool in this district to meet the needs of all learners, especially those in the more rural areas where videoconferencing often connects them with the larger schools.

Kanneken aligns well with the Professional Learning Facilitator standard as she strategically plans, provides and evaluates the impact of professional learning for educators at Prairie Rose Schools. The facilitation starts with a needs assessment through a comprehensive discussion with educators, and Kanneken then asks teachers to rate their familiarity and interest in the technology features of specific tools. The content, pace and structure of the professional development is based on that initial data. Kanneken differentiates and scaffolds learning to meet the needs of each individual educator or school leader.

> I try to provide differentiated or scaffolded learning within the session. This can take different forms. Sometimes, it might be a choice board where learners have two or three must-dos and then the rest are can-dos. If the training needs to be more linear in nature, I always insert challenge items every few minutes so that participants have an opportunity to do hands-on learning. The challenges have basic and advanced levels. This helps newer learners to not get overwhelmed, but challenges more experienced participants to explore the nooks and crannies of the tool that we might not otherwise have time to get to.
>
> — Cammie Kannekens, Instructional Coach

At the end of every professional development session, Kannekens obtains feedback data via a form, or a Flipgrid recording. Based on the feedback, she alters the learning before she supports people on that topic again and ensures she cycles back with any individuals who have questions. Shethen continues the learning to new needs and goals.

Data-Driven Decision-Maker

Kelley Briceno

Kelley Briceno is a technology integration specialist at Saint Andrew's Private School in Boca Raton, Florida. This college preparatory suburban school serves approximately 1,300 K–12 day/boarding students. Data is important to Briceno and the two other technology integration specialists she works with closely. She advocates and provides professional development to help educators understand the power behind collecting data to best drive technology to high-impact practices.

A cyclical assessment approach is used with mathematics and English teachers as diagnostic tests are administered three times a year. She works with the educator on how best to collect and use that formative and summative data to differentiate instruction. Briceno supports educators in developing their own assessments throughout the year and how to look across those data sources. In some classes, she provides professional development on how to create and implement adaptive testing. This is an assessment approach made possible by digital technologies that has the test update in real-time, directing students to a specific question or section based on the accuracy of the student's last response.

Student ownership of progress is important to Briceno, and she works with educators to empower students to use learning data to set their own goals and measure their progress. She advocates and teaches this as part of the reflection final step of the design cycle. From this process, students self-evaluate and set goals for future projects.

> Depending on the need or goal, I help educators and students navigate the intricacies of making sure their surveys are set up to gather the data they need, while providing the level of privacy and security necessary.
>
> — Kelley Briceno, Technology Integration Specialist

Laura Cahill

Laura Cahill is a district technology coach at Worcester Public School, in Massachusetts, an urban school district serving 26,000 students. Worcester Public Schools are the second largest public school district in New England and include approximately 60% of learners whose first language is not English, 20% with disabilities and 60% economically disadvantaged. Cahill assists educators and leaders in securely collecting and analyzing student data. She has educators think about how data is used to ensure that their work is purposeful and productive. She works with educators and leaders with both qualitative and quantitative data to drive toward high-impact technology integration strategies.

Cahill works closely with school leaders and educators on how to use a five-step data collection and feedback loop with students:

1. Set up the technology that will be used to gather student data.
2. Create a topic for each content standard.
3. Create an assignment to connect with each standard, including a grading scale.
4. Students complete assignments and attach evidence.
5. Educators hold a progress conference with each student, using the online gradebook as a basis for discussion.

I love data, but data is simply information. How can we, as educators, not love information about student learning to better our own practices? Being able to track trends can lead to adjusting teaching practices, and helping students to look at their own data can help them metacognitively understand more about themselves as learners, which will serve them in the future. Using digital tools for data collection makes it more readily available, easy to analyze and accessible to more people, so I enjoy helping teachers and schools set up these data systems.

— Laura Cahill, District Technology Coach

Digital Citizen Advocate

Virginia Duncan

Virginia Duncan is an instructional technology coach at Garden City High School in Garden City, Kansas. This rural high school serves approximately 2,000 students. The high school professional learning structure embeds digital citizenship and leadership within learning strategies. Incorporated into professional development are "innovation challenges" where teachers explore and implement various technology strategies and platforms in the classroom, as well as embed digital citizenship and leadership for and with students.

As part of one innovation challenge, the educator and coach worked with students to create public service announcements (PSAs) and TED-style Talks to draw connections between classroom lessons and address community issues. Students studied examples of PSAs and TEDTalks, learned about effective communication, then scripted and recorded their PSAs and TEDTalks and posted them on a classroom YouTube channel. Part of the learning process was working with students on using platforms with purpose, as well as creating a digital profile and reputation. Teachers who participated in these challenges worked with students on what and how much information should be shared, and how to use technology for an intended purpose.

Duncan also works with the educators on The 12 Days of Innovation. During one year, on Day 12, teachers were to develop interactive podcasts to record a quick learning reflection over their experience of the 12 days. Once they made their recording, they were to interact with others' recordings, promoting positive interactions with their colleagues.

Teachers were immediately planning for this activity in their own classrooms and saw how using this tool with students was a way to foster a culture of respectful online interactions. Finding where technology tools are needed instead of forcing technology for technology's sake encourages that healthy balance and ensures technology meets teachers' instructional and learning goals.

— Virginia Duncan, Instructional Technology Coach

Chad Fisher

Chad Fisher is an instructional technology coach at James Wood High School in Virginia. This rural/suburban area includes three high schools, four junior schools and 12 elementary schools. Fisher is a coach who models digital citizenship and supports educators and students in recognizing the responsibilities and opportunities inherent in living in a digital world. In recent work, he has focused on inspiring and encouraging both educators and students in using technology for civic engagement. He worked recently with one educator who wanted students to present about the impact of climate change on aquatic life.

Specifically, the goals of the assignment were to learn about providing students with an opportunity to create compelling arguments, such as public service announcements. Fisher worked with the educator to think through which digital technologies could help in this task. The focus was on the learning objectives and how technology could be used for these civic engagement tasks. Fisher advocates for a healthy balance of technology use:

> The use of technology in a classroom for the purpose of saying that a class has used technology isn't something that I like to promote. I will often tell teachers that if the process of using the technology steers a class too far away from the goal of the lesson, they should not use technology. By the same token, if the addition of some form of instructional technology will enhance the goals, then yes, it can or should be used. There needs to be a check indicator of some type for teachers and this often is where an instructional technology coach such as myself needs to step in.
>
> — Chad Fisher, Instructional Technology Coach

Some educators are nervous about the use of technology. Digital citizenship can be an unnerving topic as educators don't want students to be unsafe online. In these cases, online interactions are often avoided. Fisher partners with these teachers to build a culture of online safety and empowerment. He shows students how technology stores information that will hold them accountable for their behaviors as well as keep them safe.

> Promoting positive online engagement can and will lead toward a better digital footprint that can lead to future opportunities.
>
> — Chad Fisher, Instructional Technology Coach

Building Capacity Through Human Resources

The role of the instructional technology coach has evolved from technical support to an instructional leader who nimbly works between classrooms and schools to support teachers, while also working with leaders to develop and implement a vision for digital learning. According to the National Center on Education Statistics (NCES), there were over 66,000 full- or part-time coaches in the U.S. during the 2015–16 school year. That number continues to grow as school boards fund digital learning initiatives.

Human resources leaders are using the ISTE Standards for Coaches as their job description, much like Prosper Independent School District did when it was hiring new instructional technology coaches.

JOB DESCRIPTION TEMPLATE
Educational Technology Coach/Instructional Technology Coach

POSITION PURPOSE

The role of the Educational Technology Coach/Instructional Technology Coach is to establish collaborative, effective partnerships with teaching staff and leaders to use technology for high-quality learning and implement the district vision; plan, provide and evaluate professional learning that improves use of technology for teaching; model and support individual educators to design learning experiences that meet the needs of all students; partner with leaders and educators to identify and evaluate the efficacy of digital learning content and tools; and model and promote digital citizenship.

MINIMUM QUALIFICATION GUIDELINES

- Certified teacher with three years teaching experience.
- Demonstration of competency in the ISTE Standards for Educators (e.g., earning ISTE Certification for Educators).
- Working knowledge of the ISTE Standards for Coaches.

SKILL REQUIREMENTS

- Demonstrated leadership skills
- Excellent communication skills, including crucial conversations.
- Strong presentation, planning and evaluation skills.
- Exemplary working knowledge of a wide range of digital tools and resources for learning.
- Demonstrated evidence of continuous learning and improvement.

Continued

MAJOR RESPONSIBILITIES

1. Change Agent

Coaches inspire educators and leaders to use technology to create equitable and ongoing access to high-quality learning. Coaches:

a. Create a shared vision and culture for using technology to learn and accelerate transformation through the coaching process.

b. Facilitate equitable use of digital learning tools and content that meet the needs of each learner.

c. Cultivate a supportive coaching culture that encourages educators and leaders to achieve a shared vision and individual goals.

d. Recognize educators across the organization who use technology effectively to enable high-impact teaching and learning.

e. Connect leaders, educators, instructional support, technical support, domain experts and solution providers to maximize the potential of technology for learning.

2. Connected Learner

Coaches model the ISTE Standards for Students and the ISTE Standards for Educators, and identify ways to improve their coaching practice. Coaches:

a. Pursue professional learning that deepens expertise in the ISTE Standards in order to serve as a model for educators and leaders.

b. Actively participate in professional learning networks to enhance coaching practice and keep current with emerging technology and innovations in pedagogy and the learning sciences.

c. Establish shared goals with educators, reflect on successes and continually improve coaching and teaching practice.

3. Collaborator

Coaches establish productive relationships with educators in order to improve instructional practice and learning outcomes. Coaches:

a. Establish trusting and respectful coaching relationships that encourage educators to explore new instructional strategies.

b. Partner with educators to identify digital learning content that is culturally relevant, developmentally appropriate and aligned to content standards.

c. Partner with educators to evaluate the efficacy of digital learning content and tools to inform procurement decisions and adoption.

d. Personalize support for educators by planning and modeling the effective use of technology to improve student learning.

Continued

4. Learning Designer

Coaches model and support educators to design learning experiences and environments to meet the needs and interests of all students. Coaches:

a. Collaborate with educators to develop authentic, active learning experiences that foster student agency, deepen content mastery and allow students to demonstrate their competency.

b. Help educators use digital tools to create effective assessments that provide timely feedback and support personalized learning.

c. Collaborate with educators to design accessible and active digital learning environments that accommodate learner variability.

d. Model the use of instructional design principles with educators to create effective digital learning environments.

5. Professional Learning Facilitator

Coaches plan, provide and evaluate the impact of professional learning for educators and leaders to use technology to advance teaching and learning. Coaches:

a. Design professional learning based on needs assessments and frameworks for working with adults to support their cultural, social-emotional and learning needs.

b. Build the capacity of educators, leaders and instructional teams to put the ISTE Standards into practice by facilitating active learning and providing meaningful feedback.

c. Evaluate the impact of professional learning and continually make improvements in order to meet the schoolwide vision for using technology for high-impact teaching and learning.

6. Data-Driven Decision-Maker

Coaches model and support the use of qualitative and quantitative data to inform their own instruction and professional learning. Coaches:

a. Assist educators and leaders in securely collecting and analyzing student data.

b. Support educators to interpret qualitative and quantitative data to inform their decisions and support individual student learning.

c. Partner with educators to empower students to use learning data to set their own goals and measure their progress.

7. Digital Citizen Advocate

Coaches model digital citizenship and support educators and students in recognizing the responsibilities and opportunities inherent in living in a digital world. Coaches:

a. Inspire and encourage educators and students to use technology for civic engagement and to address challenges to improve their communities.

b. Partner with educators, leaders, students and families to foster a culture of respectful online interactions and a healthy balance in their use of technology.

c. Support educators and students to critically examine the sources of online media and identify underlying assumptions.

d. Empower educators, leaders and students to make informed decisions to protect their personal data and curate the digital profile they intend to reflect.

References and Credits

References

Corwin. (2018). One-to-one coaching cycle. Retrieved from https://us.corwin.com/en-us/nam/coaching-cycle-what-does-it-look-like

Crompton, H., Olszewski, B., & Bielefeldt, T. (2016). The mobile learning training needs of educators in technology-enabled environments. *Professional Development in Education 42*(3), 482-501.

EL Education. (2015). Instructional coaching cycles in EL schools. Retrieved from file: ///D:/Downloads/ELED-CoachingCycles-0815.pdf

Eisenberg, E., Eisenberg, B., Medrich, E., & Charner, I. (2017). *Instructional Coaching in Action: An Integrated Approach That Transforms Thinking, Practice, and Schools*. ASCD: Alexandria, VA.

Knight, J. (2018). *The impact cycle: What instructional coaches should do to foster powerful improvements in teaching*. Thousand Oaks, CA: Corwin, SAGE.

Mandinach, E. B. & Gummer, E. S. What does it mean for teachers to be data literate: Laying out the skills, knowledge, and dispositions. *Teaching and Teacher Education 60*, 366-376.

Rivera, N., Burley, K., & Sass, J. (February, 2004). Evaluation of school-based professional development (2002-03). Los Angeles Unified School District, Planning, Assessment, and Research Division Publication No. 187. Retrieved from http://notebook.lausd.net/pls/ptl/url/ITEM/DC60153W2670EBA0E033081FB5EBA

Wesely, P. M., & Plummer, E. (2017). Situated learning for foreign language teachers in one-to-one computing initiatives. *CALICO Journal, 34*(2), 178-195.

Credits

Booklet Author

Helen Crompton

Standards Development Team

Richard Culatta, Chief Executive Officer
Joseph South, Chief Learning Officer
Carolyn Sykora, Senior Director of ISTE Standards Programs

Standards Technical Working Group

Clara Alaniz, Digital Learning Specialist, Plano Independent School District
M. Cristina Escobar, Director, AULA Activa, Chile
Gregory Gilmore, Instructional Technology Coach, Osage Trail Middle School
Miguel Guhlin, Director of Professional Development, Texas Computer Education Association (TCEA)
Mary Howard, Teacher, Grand Island Public Schools
Ruth Okoye, Director of K–12 Initiatives, The Source for Learning
Traci Redish, Chair, Kennesaw State University
James Centeno, Instructional Coach, Los Angeles Unified School District